EASY GUITAR WITH NOTES & TAB

CHART HITS OF 2020-2021

ISBN 978-1-7051-3362-0

HAL•LEONARD®

Visit Hal Leonard Online at
www.halleonard.com

Contact us:
Hal Leonard
7777 West Bluemound Road
Milwaukee, WI 53213
Email: info@halleonard.com

In Europe, contact:
Hal Leonard Europe Limited
42 Wigmore Street
Marylebone, London, W1U 2RN
Email: info@halleonardeurope.com

In Australia, contact:
Hal Leonard Australia Pty. Ltd.
4 Lentara Court
Cheltenham, Victoria, 3192 Australia
Email: info@halleonard.com.au

STRUM AND PICK PATTERNS

This chart contains the suggested strum and pick patterns that are referred to by number at the beginning of each song in this book. The symbols ⊓ and ∨ in the strum patterns refer to down and up strokes, respectively. The letters in the pick patterns indicate which right-hand fingers play which strings.

p = thumb
i = index finger
m = middle finger
a = ring finger

For example; Pick Pattern 2
is played: thumb - index - middle - ring

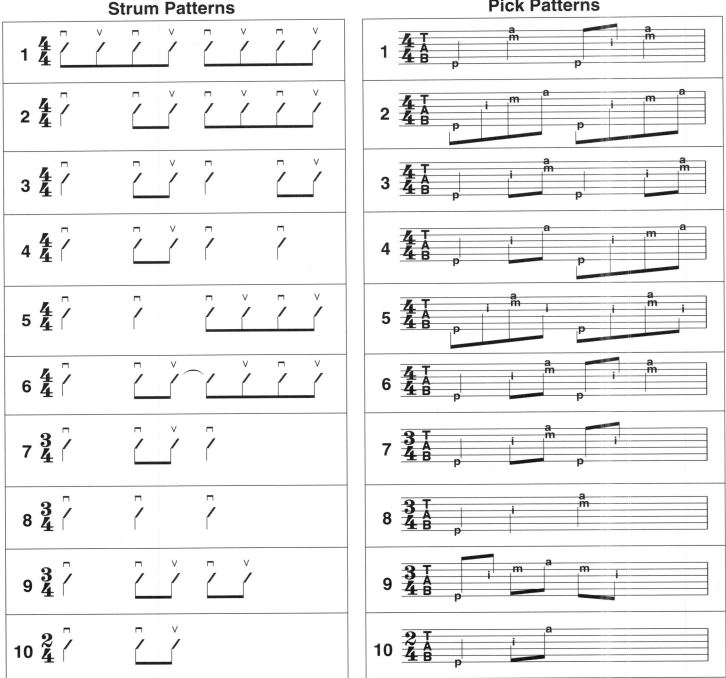

Strum Patterns   ### Pick Patterns

You can use the 3/4 Strum and Pick Patterns in songs written in compound meter (6/8, 9/8, 12/8, etc.). For example, you can accompany a song in 6/8 by playing the 3/4 pattern twice in each measure. The 4/4 Strum and Pick Patterns can be used for songs written in cut time (¢) by doubling the note time values in the patterns. Each pattern would therefore last two measures in cut time.

Diamonds

Words and Music by Sam Smith, Oscar Gorres and Shellback

*Capo 1

Strum Pattern: 1, 4
Pick Pattern: 2, 5

Moderately

1. Have it all.

*Optional: To match recording, place capo at 1st fret.

Verse

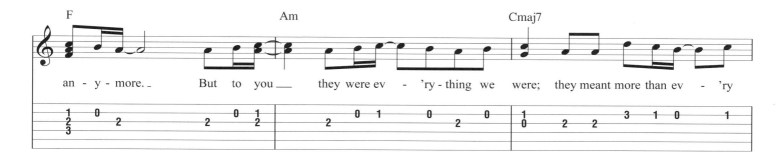

Rip our mem-'ries off the wall.__ All the spe-cial things I bought, they mean noth-ing to __ me

an-y-more.__ But to you __ they were ev-'ry-thing we were; they meant more than ev-'ry

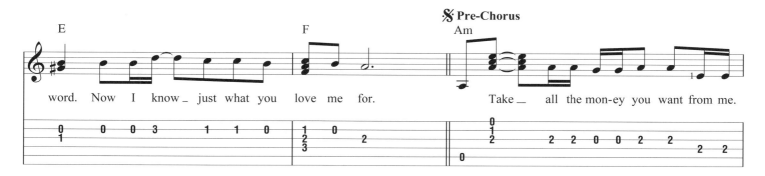

word. Now I know __ just what you love me for.

Pre-Chorus

Take __ all the mon-ey you want from me.

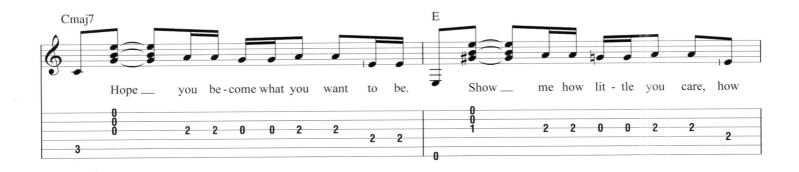

Cmaj7 / E

Hope ___ you be-come what you want to be. Show ___ me how lit-tle you care, how

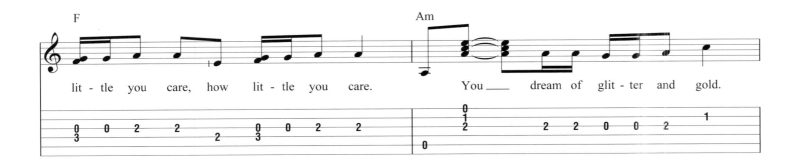

F / Am

lit - tle you care, how lit - tle you care. You ___ dream of glit - ter and gold.

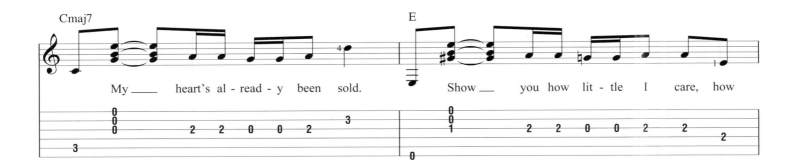

Cmaj7 / E

My ___ heart's al-read - y been sold. Show ___ you how lit - tle I care, how

F / N.C.

lit - tle I care, how lit - tle I care. ___ My dia - monds leave with

Chorus

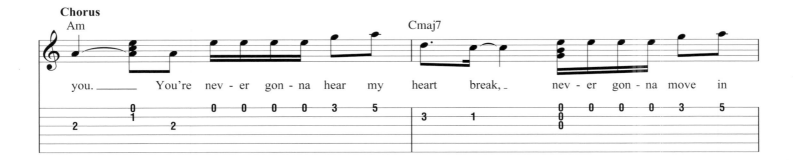

Am / Cmaj7

you. ___ You're nev - er gon - na hear my heart break, ___ nev - er gon - na move in

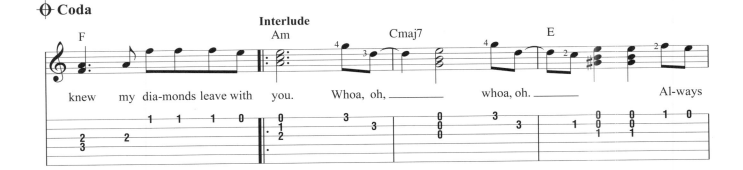

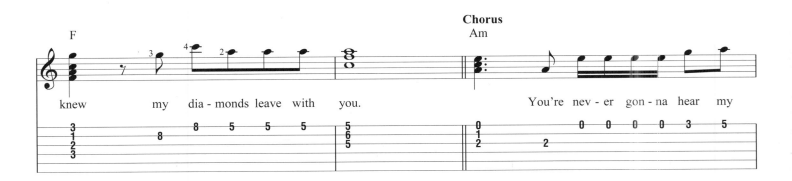

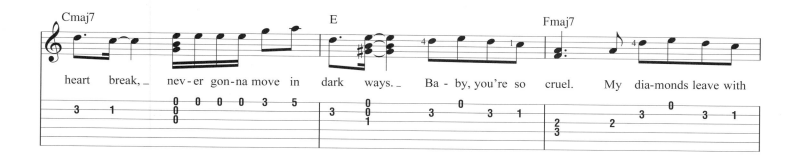

heart break, _ nev-er gon-na move in dark ways. _ Ba - by, you're so cruel. My dia-monds leave with

you. _ Ma - te - ri - al love won't fool me. _ When you're not here I can breathe. _ Think I al - ways

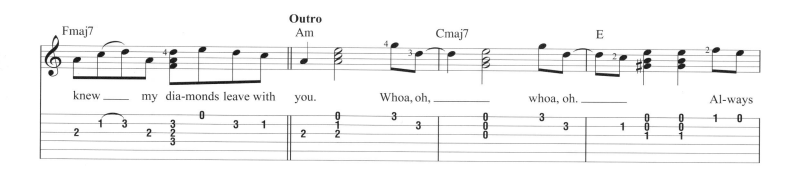

Outro

knew _ my dia-monds leave with you. Whoa, oh, _ whoa, oh. _ Al-ways

knew my dia-monds leave with you. _ Whoa, oh, _ whoa, oh. _ Al-ways

knew my dia-monds leave with you.

Afterglow

Words and Music by Ed Sheeran, David Hodges and Fred Gibson

*Capo IV

Strum Pattern: 6
Pick Pattern: 4, 6

Verse
Moderately

1. Stop the clocks; it's a-maz - ing.
2. The weath-er out-side's ___ chang - ing.

*Optional: To match recording, place capo at the 4th fret.

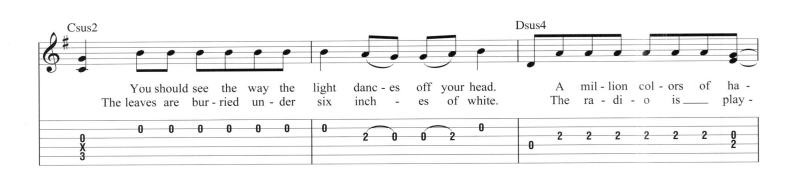

You should see the way the light danc-es off your head.
The leaves are bur-ried un-der six inch-es of white.

A mil-lion col-ors of ha-
The ra-di-o is ___ play-

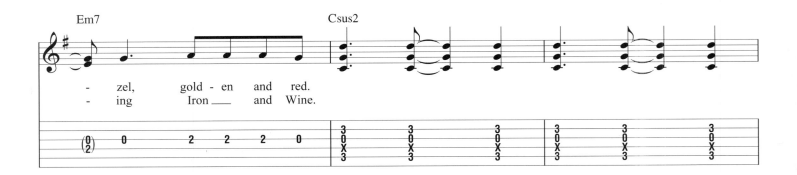

- zel, gold-en and red.
- ing Iron ___ and Wine.

Sat - ur - day morn - ing is fad - ing.
This is a new di - men - sion,

The sun's re - flect - ed by the
this is a lev - el where we're

cof - fee in your hand.
los - ing track of time.

My eyes are caught in your gaze
I'm hold - ing noth - ing a - gainst

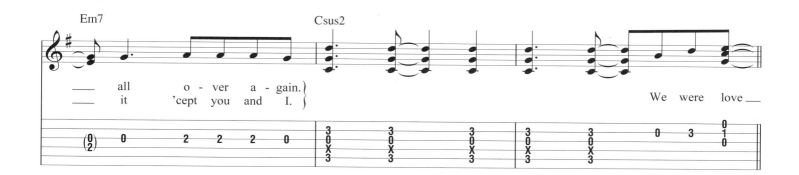

all o - ver a - gain.
it 'cept you and I.

We were love

Chorus

drunk, wait - ing on a mir - a - cle, tryin' to find our - selves in the

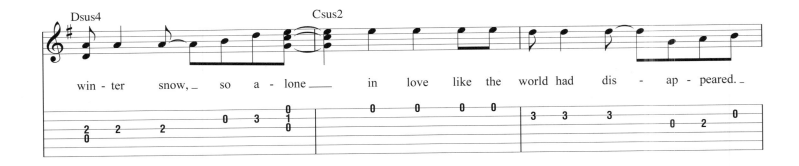

win - ter snow, _ so a - lone _ in love like the world had dis - ap - peared. _

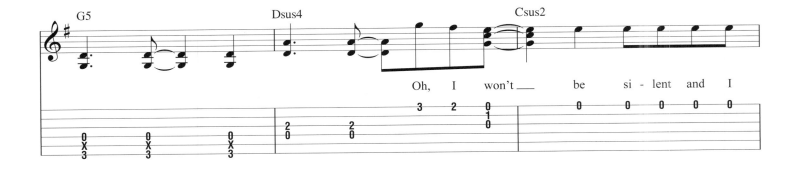

Oh, I won't _ be si - lent and I

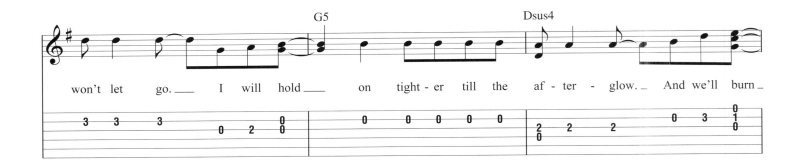

won't let go. _ I will hold _ on tight - er till the af - ter - glow. _ And we'll burn _

_ so bright till the dark - ness soft - ly clears. _

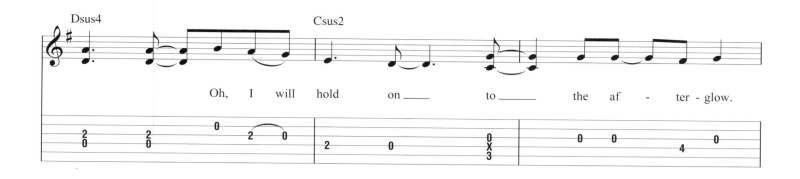

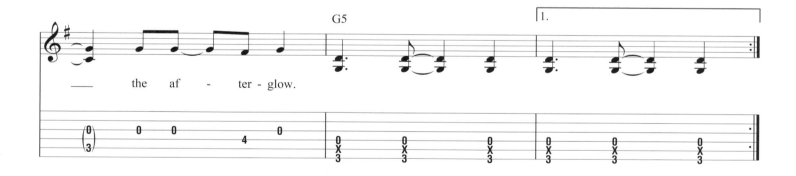

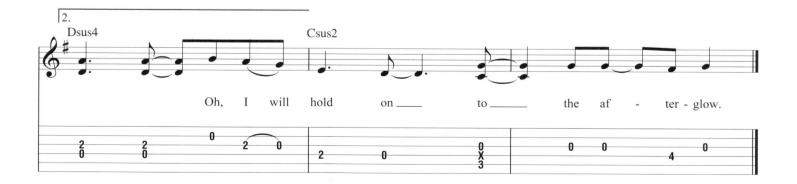

Anyone

Words and Music by Justin Bieber, Jon Bellion, Jordan Johnson, Alexander Izquierdo,
Andrew Watt, Raul Cubina, Stefan Johnson and Michael Pollack

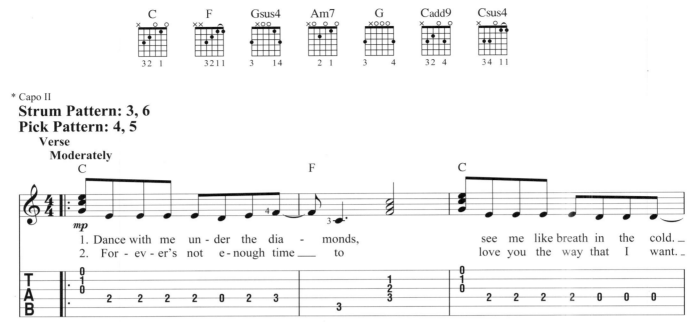

* Capo II

Strum Pattern: 3, 6
Pick Pattern: 4, 5

Verse
Moderately

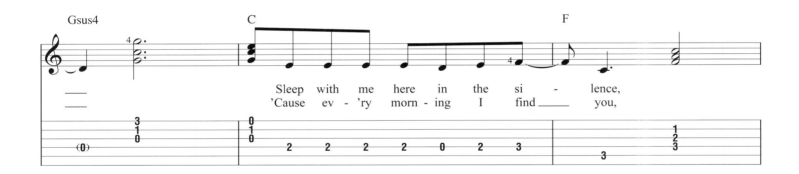

1. Dance with me un-der the dia-monds, see me like breath in the cold.
2. For-ev-er's not e-nough time to love you the way that I want.

*Optional: To match recording, place capo at 2nd fret.

Sleep with me here in the si-lence,
'Cause ev-'ry morn-ing I find you,

come kiss me sil-ver and gold.
I fear the day that I don't.

You say that I won't lose you, but you can't
You say that I won`t lose you, but you can't

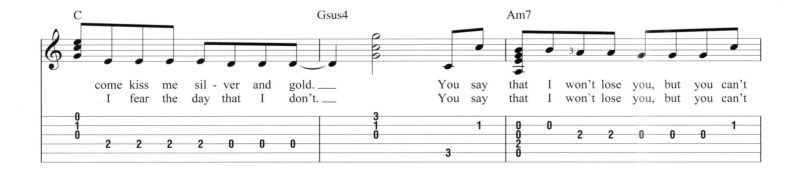

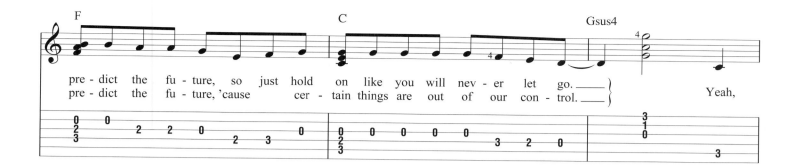

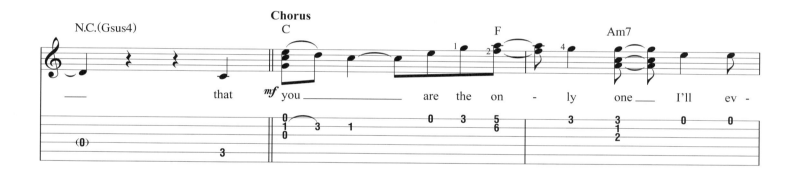

_____ on my life, _____ you're the on - ly good _____ I've ev - er done. _____ (Ev -

er done.) _____ Ee - yeah, you, _____ if it's not _____ you, it's _____ not an -

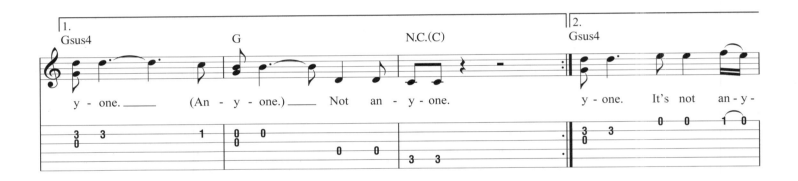

1.
y - one. _____ (An - y - one.) _____ Not an - y - one. _____ **2.** y - one. It's not an - y -

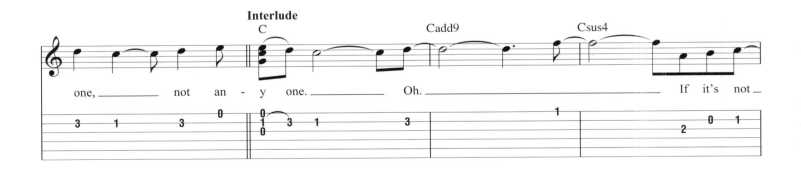

Interlude

one, _____ not an - y one. _____ Oh. _____ If it's not _____

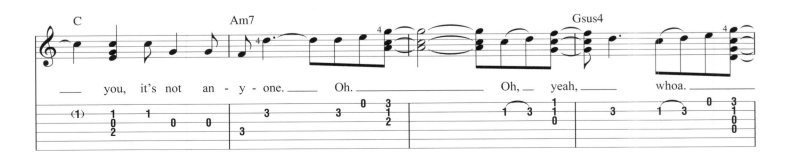

_____ you, it's not an - y - one. _____ Oh. _____ Oh, _____ yeah, _____ whoa. _____

Outro-Chorus

Drivers License

Words and Music by Daniel Nigro and Olivia Rodrigo

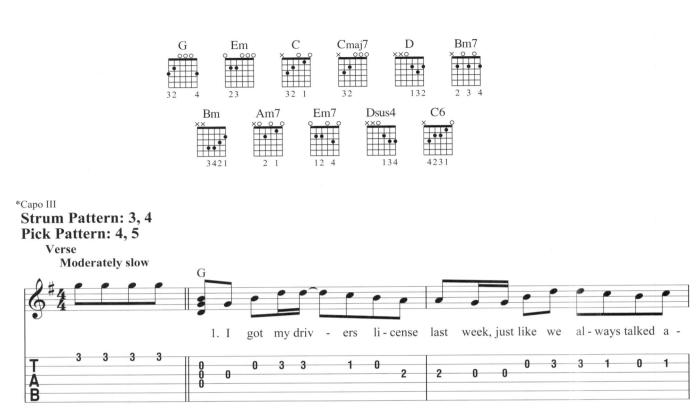

*Capo III

Strum Pattern: 3, 4
Pick Pattern: 4, 5

Verse
Moderately slow

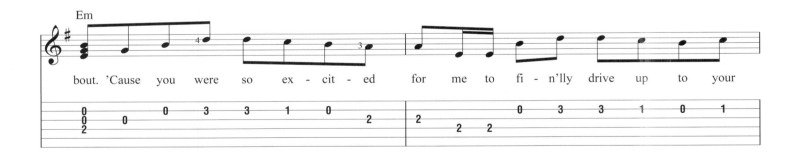

1. I got my drivers license last week, just like we al-ways talked a-

*Optional: To match recording, place capo at 3rd fret.

bout. 'Cause you were so ex-cit-ed for me to fi-n'lly drive up to your

house. But to-day I drove through the sub-urbs, cry-ing 'cause you weren't a-

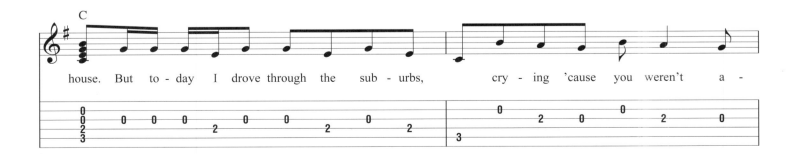

round.   2. And you're prob-'ly with the blond girl   who al-ways made me doubt.

She's so much old-er than me; she's ev-'ry-thing I'm in-se-cure a-bout. Yeah, to-

day I drove through the sub-urbs,   'cause how could I   ev-er love some-one else?   And

I know we weren't per-fect, but I've nev-er felt this way   for no one.   And

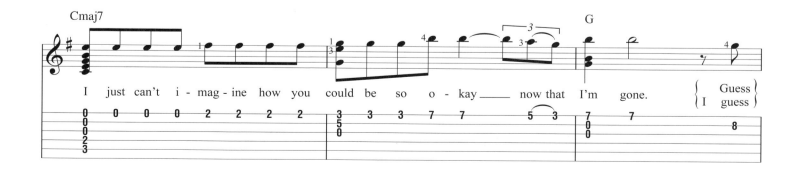

I just can't i-mag-ine how you could be so o-kay   now that I'm gone.   { Guess } { I guess }

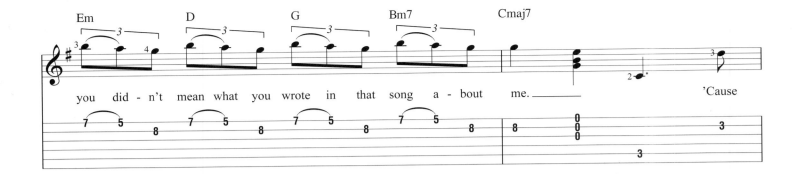

you did-n't mean what you wrote in that song a-bout me._____ 'Cause

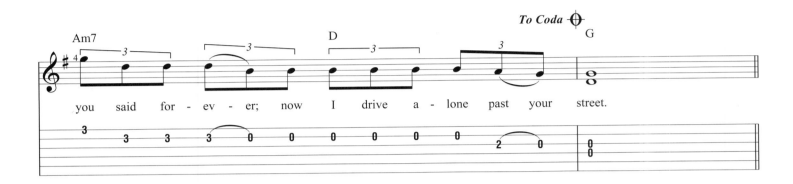

you said for-ev-er; now I drive a-lone past your street.

Verse

3. And all my friends are tired.___ of hear-ing how much I miss you; but

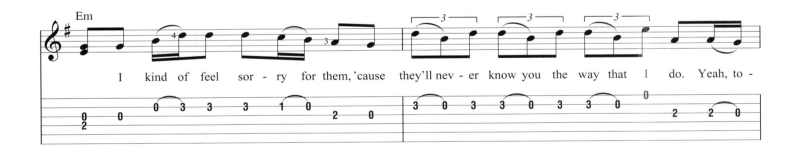

I kind of feel sor-ry for them, 'cause they'll nev-er know you the way that I do. Yeah, to-

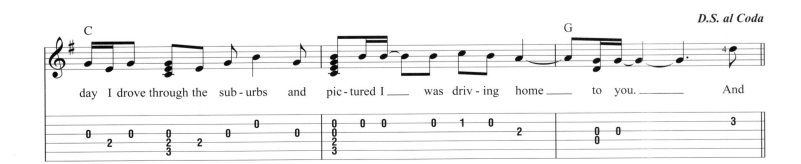

day I drove through the sub-urbs and pic-tured I ___ was driv-ing home ___ to you. And

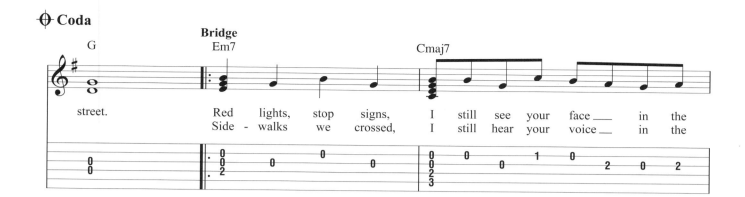

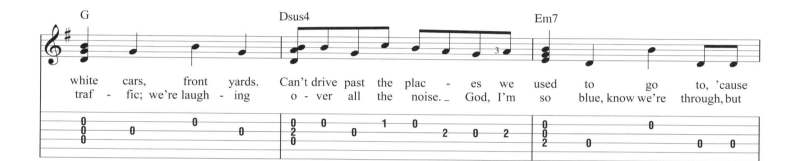

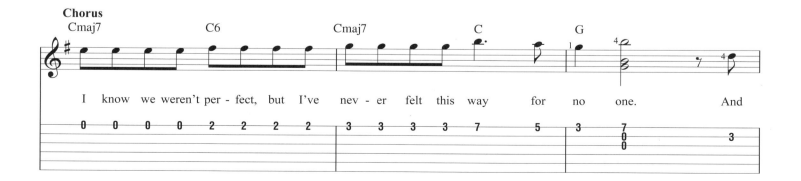

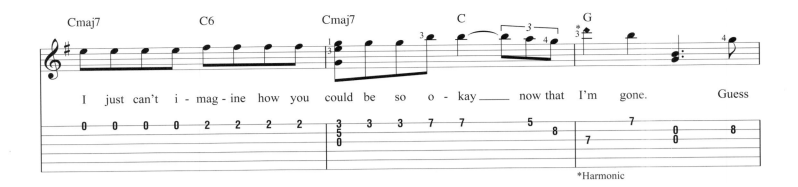

I just can't i-mag-ine how you could be so o-kay___ now that I'm gone. Guess

*Harmonic

you did-n't mean what you wrote in that song a-bout me. 'Cause

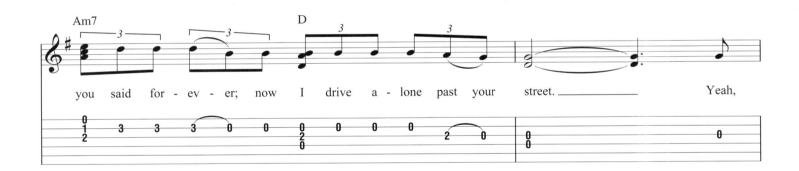

you said for-ev-er; now I drive a-lone past your street.___ Yeah,

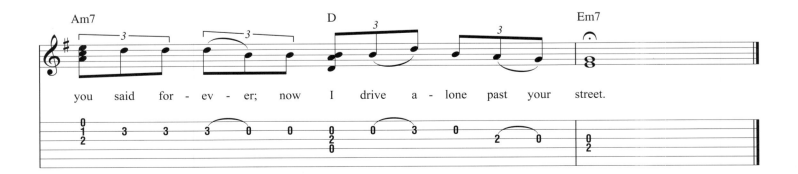

you said for-ev-er; now I drive a-lone past your street.

Dynamite

Words and Music by Jessica Agombar and David Stewart

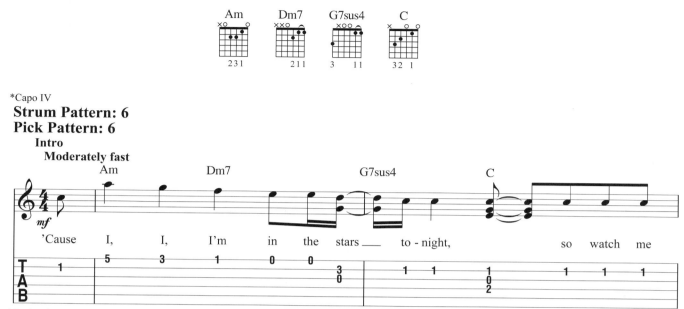

*Capo IV

Strum Pattern: 6
Pick Pattern: 6

Intro
Moderately fast

'Cause I, I, I'm in the stars ___ to-night, so watch me

*Optional: To match recording, place capo at 4th fret.

bring the fire, set the night ___ a-light.

Verse

1. Show's on, I get up in the morn, cup of

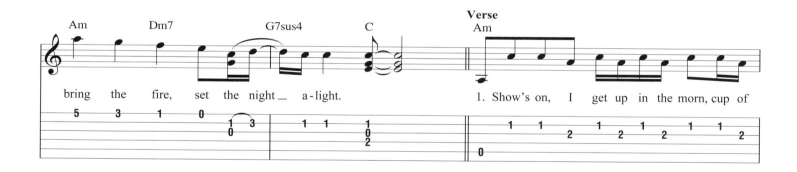

milk, let's rock and roll. King Kong, kick the drum, ___ roll-ing on like a Roll-ing Stone.

Sing song when I'm walk-ing home, _ jump up to the top, Le-Bron. Ding-dong, call me on my phone, iced

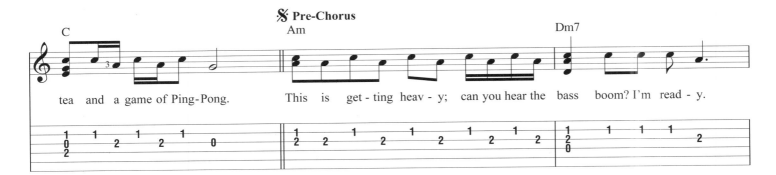

𝄋 Pre-Chorus

tea and a game of Ping-Pong. This is get-ting heav-y; can you hear the bass boom? I'm read-y.

Life is sweet as hon-ey, yeah, this beat, cha-ching _ like mon-ey. Dis-co o-ver-load _ I'm

in-to that; _ I'm good to go. _ I'm dia-mond; you know I glow _ up. {Hey, so let's go! / Hey, let's go!} 'Cause

Chorus

I, I, I'm in the stars to-night, so watch me bring the fire, set the night _

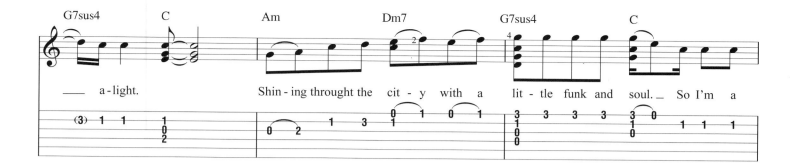

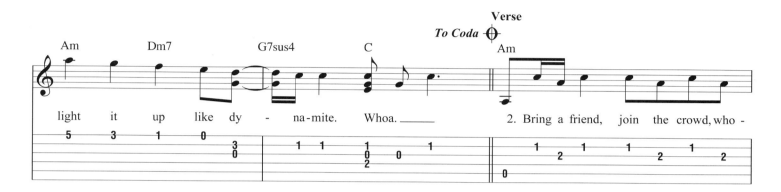

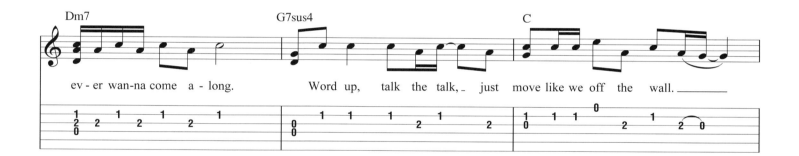

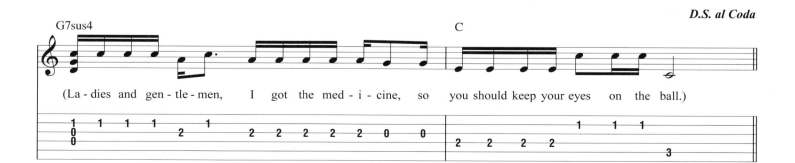

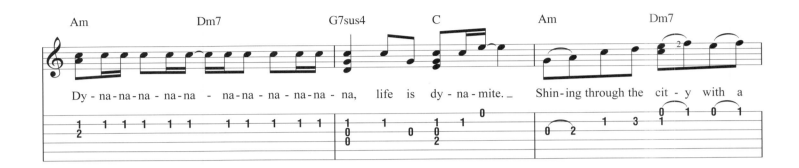

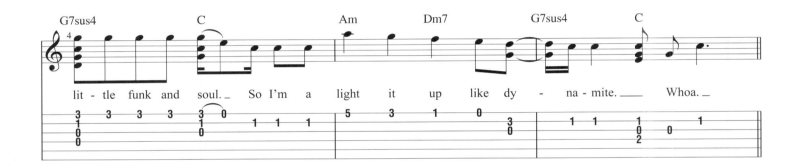

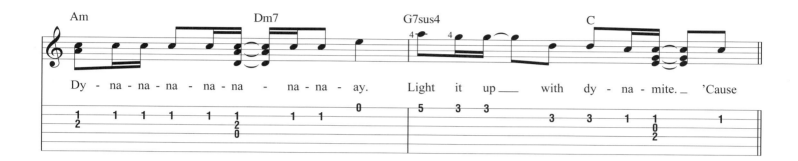

Outro

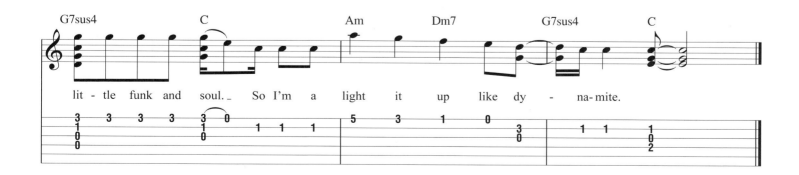

Forever After All

Words and Music by Drew Parker, Robert Williford and Luke Combs

Strum Pattern: 6
Pick Pattern: 4

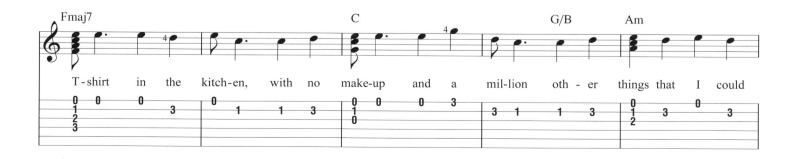

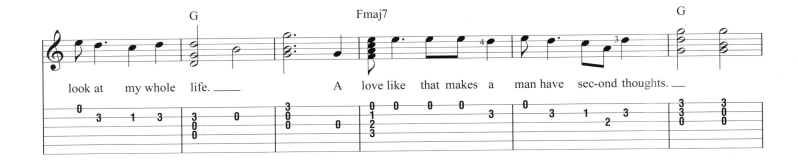

look at my whole life. ___ A love like that makes a man have sec-ond thoughts. ___

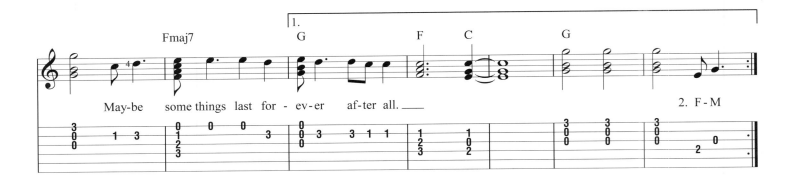

May-be some things last for - ev - er af-ter all. ___ 2. F - M

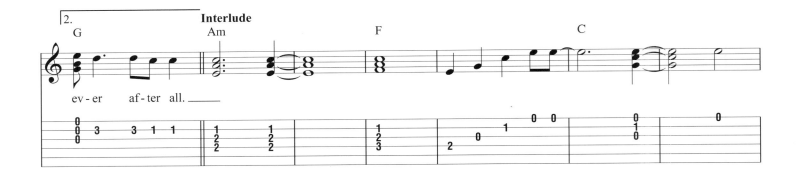

ev - er af-ter all. ___

Outro-Chorus

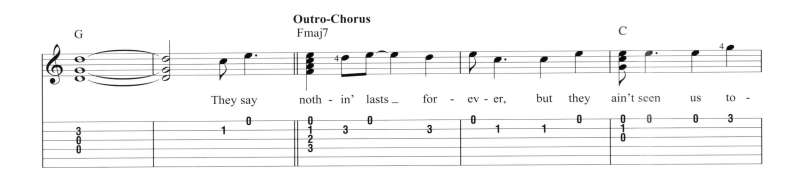

They say noth - in' lasts ___ for - ev - er, but they ain't seen us to -

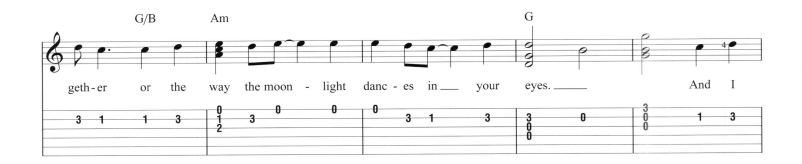

geth - er or the way the moon - light danc - es in ___ your eyes. ___ And I

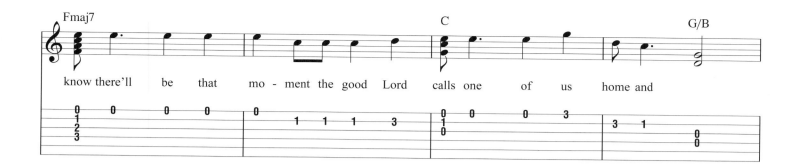

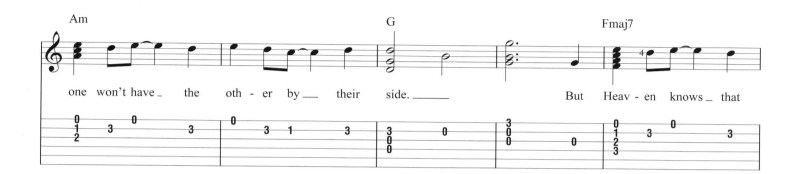

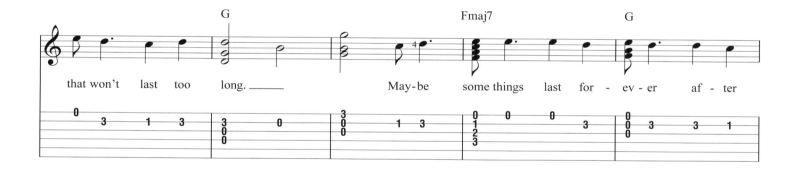

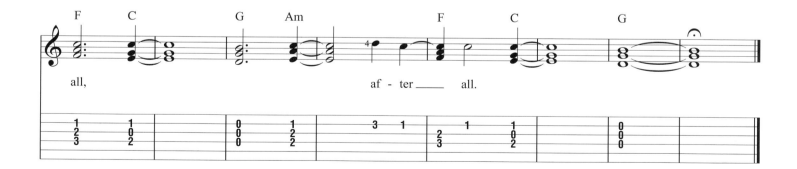

Additional Lyrics

2. FM station on the outskirts,
   Blue jeans after years of shift work,
   All fadin' out like I always knew they would.
   The strings on this guitar,
   The first love lost on a young heart,
   Those things are gonna break after the gettin's good.

Happy Anywhere

Words and Music by Ross Copperman, Josh Osborne and Matt Jenkins

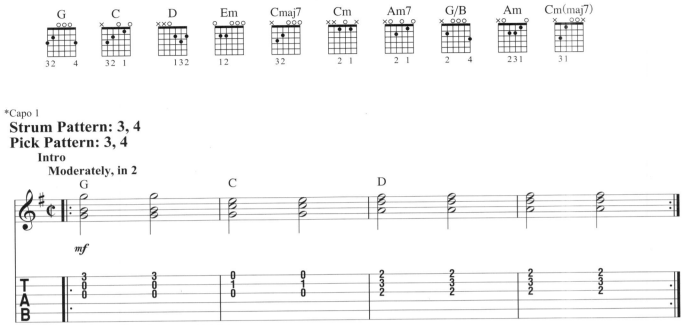

*Capo 1

Strum Pattern: 3, 4
Pick Pattern: 3, 4

Intro
Moderately, in 2

*Optional: To match recording, place capo at 1st fret.

Verse

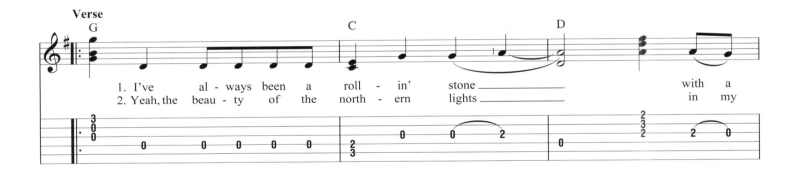

1. I've always been a rollin' stone _____ with a
2. Yeah, the beauty of the northern lights _____ in my

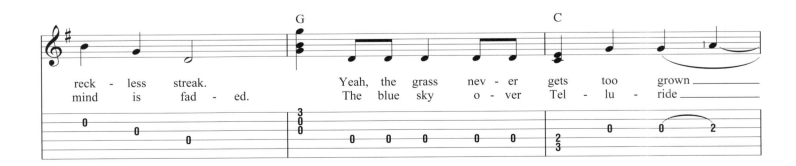

reck-less streak. Yeah, the grass nev-er gets too grown _____
mind is fad-ed. The blue sky o-ver Tel-lu-ride _____

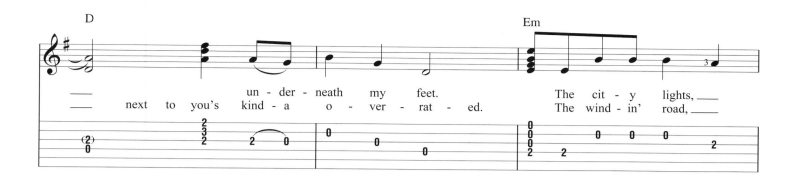

un - der - neath my feet. The cit - y lights, ____

next to you's kind - a o - ver - rat - ed. The wind - in' road, ____

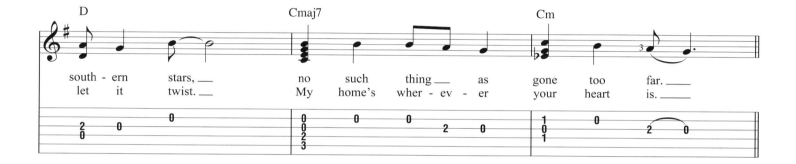

south - ern stars, ____ no such thing ____ as gone too far. ____

let it twist. ____ My home's wher - ev - er your heart is. ____

%Chorus

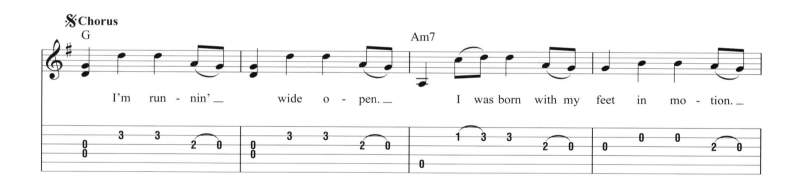

I'm run - nin' __ wide o - pen. __ I was born with my feet in mo - tion. __

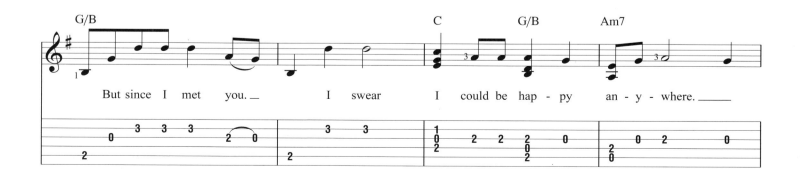

But since I met you. __ I swear I could be hap - py an - y - where. ____

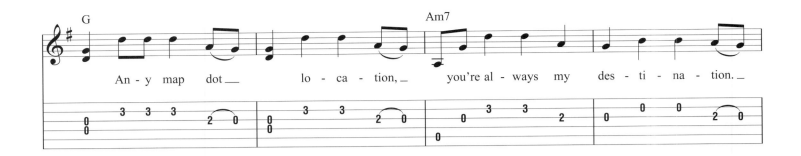

An - y map dot __ lo - ca - tion, __ you're al - ways my des - ti - na - tion. __

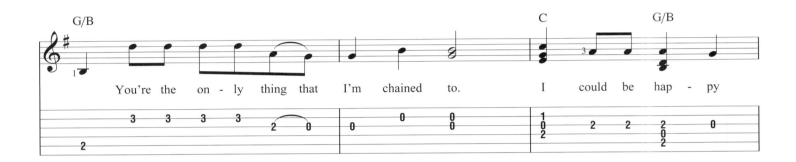

You're the on - ly thing that I'm chained to. I could be hap - py

To Coda

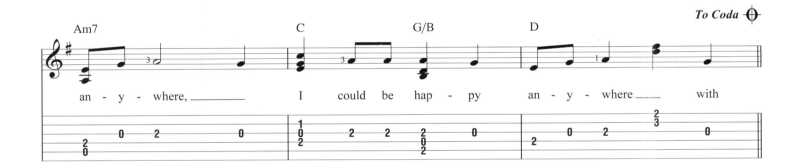

an - y - where, _____ I could be hap - py an - y - where ____ with

1. **Interlude**

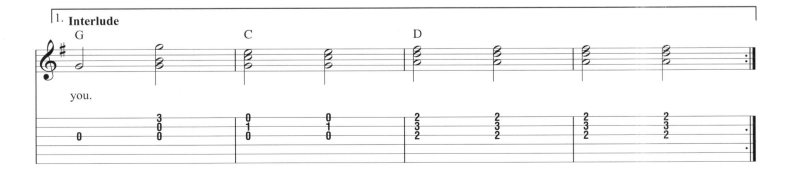

you.

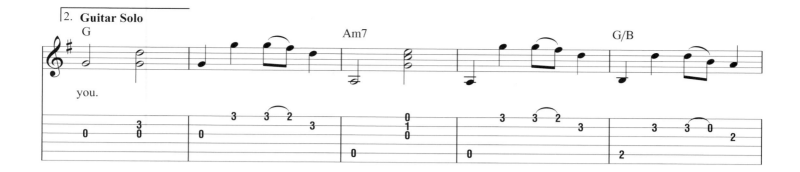

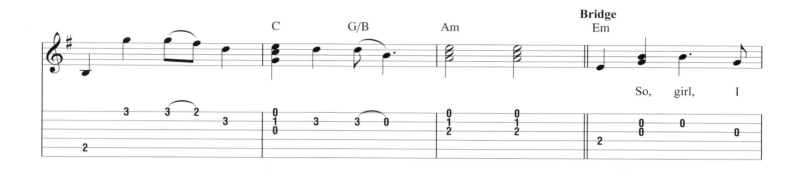

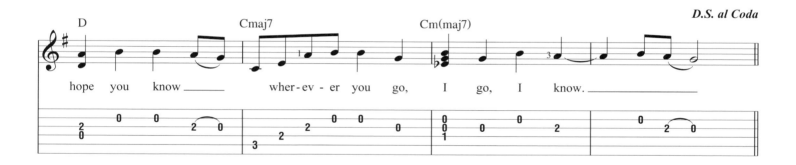

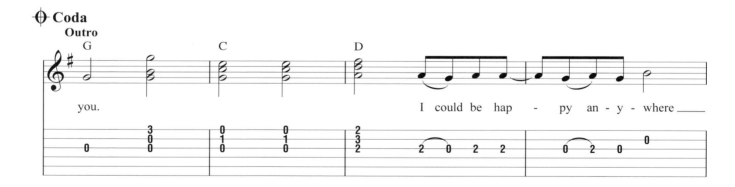

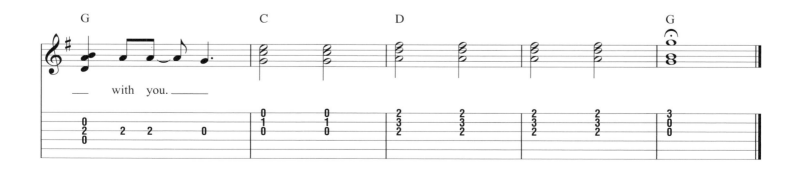

Monster

Words and Music by Justin Bieber, Shawn Mendes,
Mustafa Ahmed, Adam Feeney and Ashton Simmonds

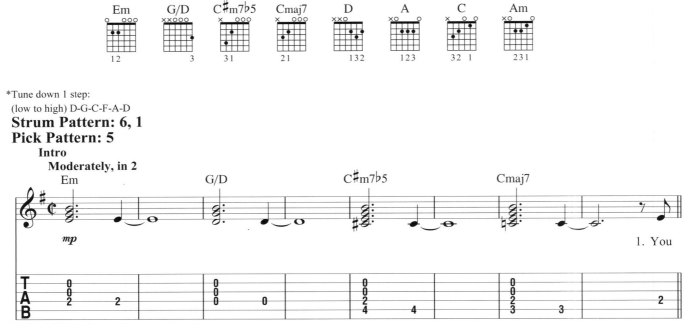

*Tune down 1 step:
(low to high) D-G-C-F-A-D

Strum Pattern: 6, 1
Pick Pattern: 5

Intro
Moderately, in 2

*Optional: To match recording, tune down 1 step.

Verse
N.C.

put me on a ped-es-tal and tell me I'm the best. __

Raise me up in-to the sky un-til I'm short of breath. __

Fill me up with con - fi - dence, I say what's in my chest. ___ Spill my words and tear me down un -

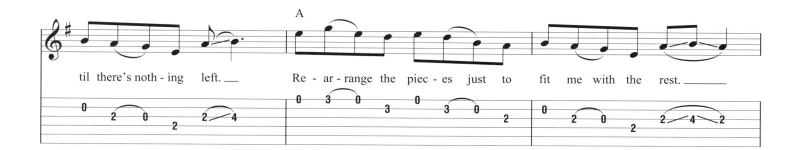

til there's noth - ing left. ___ Re - ar - range the piec - es just to fit me with the rest._____

𝄋 **Chorus**

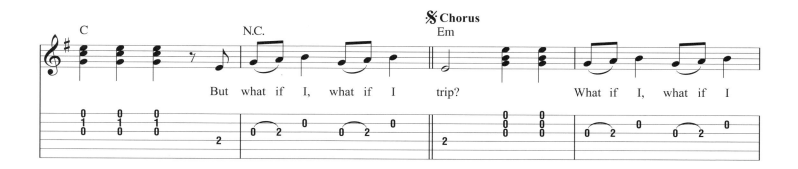

But what if I, what if I trip? What if I, what if I

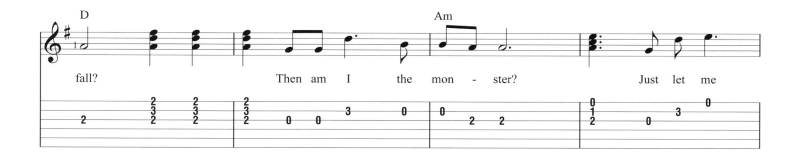

fall? Then am I the mon - ster? Just let me

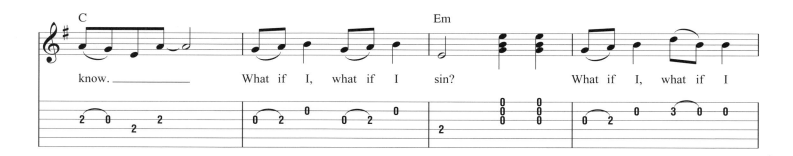

know. _____ What if I, what if I sin? What if I, what if I

ev-'ry-thing I've done. Hold-ing it a-gainst me like you're the ho-ly one.

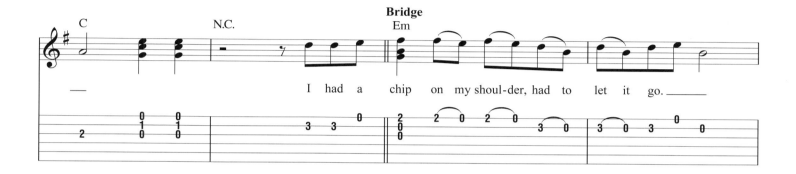

I had a chip on my shoul-der, had to let it go.

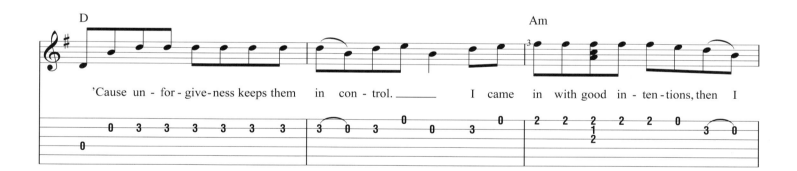

'Cause un-for-give-ness keeps them in con-trol. I came in with good in-ten-tions, then I

D.S. al Coda

let it go. And now I real-ly want to know. What if I

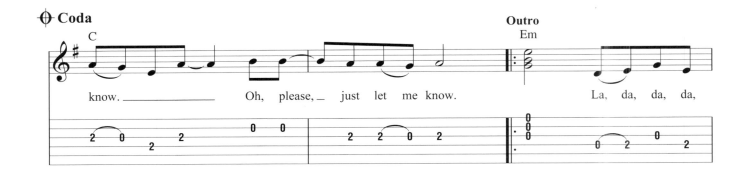

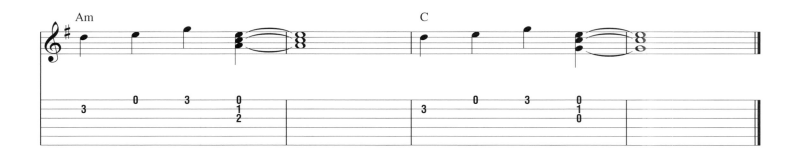

Surrender

Words and Music by Natalie Ann Howard and Jonathan Michael Howard

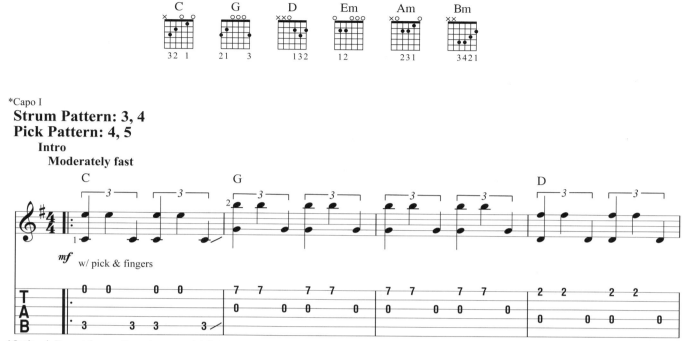

*Capo I

Strum Pattern: 3, 4

Pick Pattern: 4, 5

Intro

Moderately fast

mf w/ pick & fingers

*Optional: To match recording, place capo 1st fret.

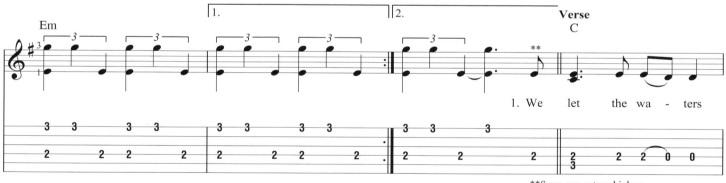

1. We let the wa - ters

**Sung one octave higher.

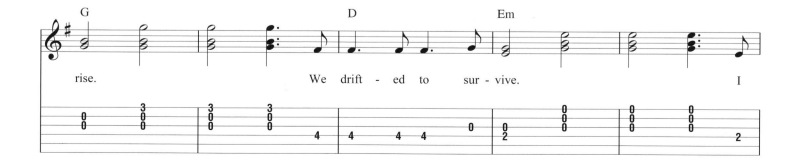

rise. We drift - ed to sur - vive.

needed you to stay, but I let you drift away. My

Pre-Chorus

love, where are you? My love where are you? When-

Chorus

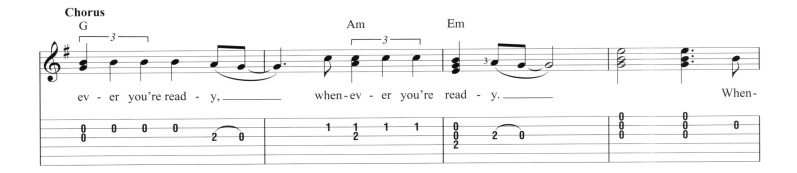

ev-er you're read-y, when-ev-er you're read-y. When-

ev-er you're read-y, when-ev-er you're read-y. Can we,

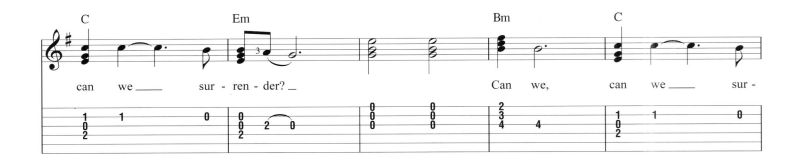

can we sur-ren-der? Can we, can we sur-

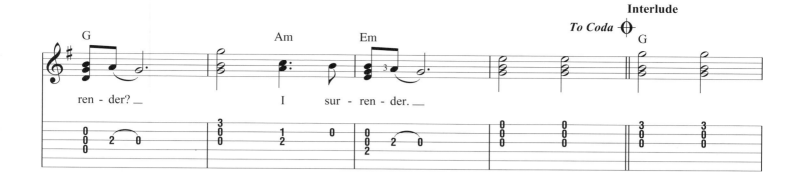

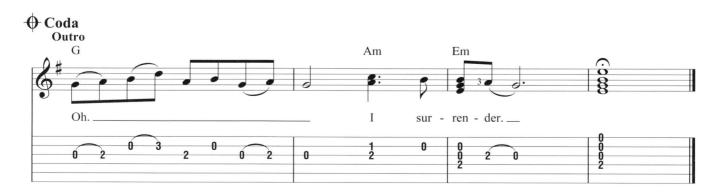

Starting Over

Words and Music by Chris Stapleton and Mike Henderson

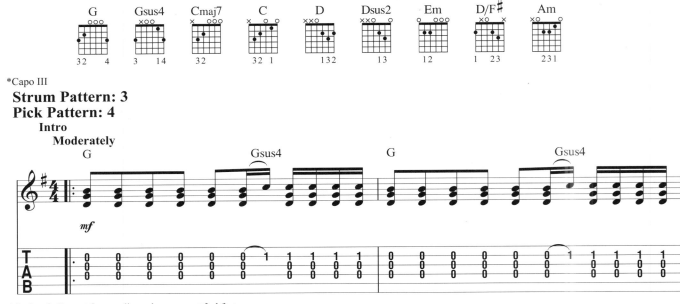

*Capo III

Strum Pattern: 3
Pick Pattern: 4

Intro
Moderately

*Optional: To match recording, place capo at 3rd fret.

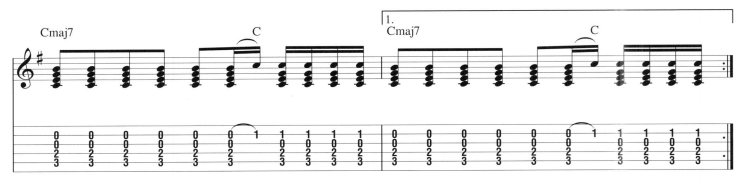

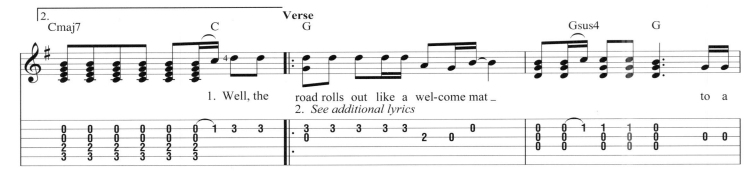

1. Well, the road rolls out like a wel-come mat _ to a
2. *See additional lyrics*

bet-ter place than the one we're at.   And I ain't got no kind of plan, _____

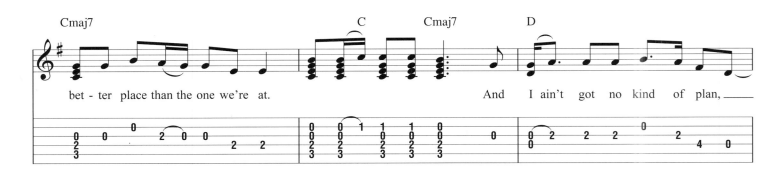

but I've had all of this town I can stand. And

I got friends out on the coast. We can jump in the wa-ter and see what floats.

We've been sav-in' for a rain-y day.

Let's beat this storm and be on our way. And

𝄋 Chorus

it don't mat-ter to me; wher-ev-er we are is where I wan-na be. And,

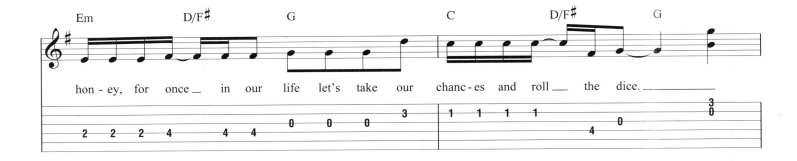

hon - ey, for once __ in our life let's take our chanc - es and roll __ the dice. __

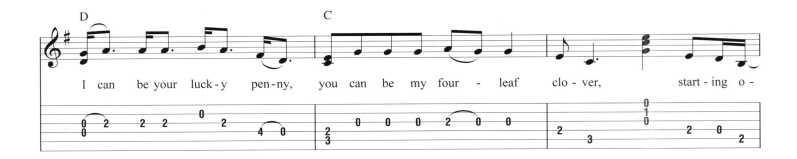

I can be your luck - y pen - ny, you can be my four - leaf clo - ver, start - ing o -

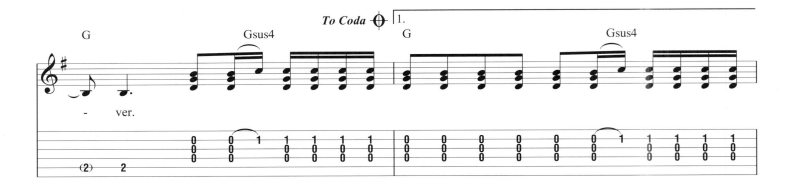

To Coda ✛ | 1.

- ver.

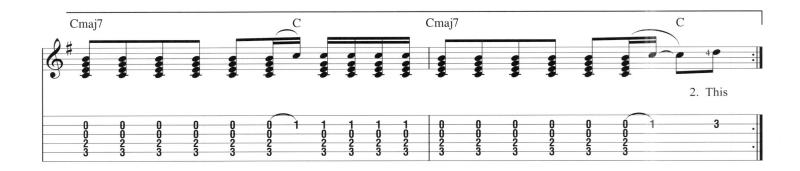

2. This

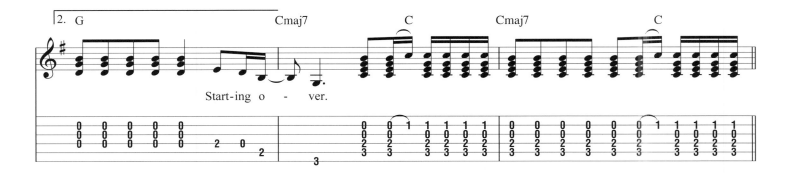

2. Start - ing o - ver.

Interlude

D.S. al Coda

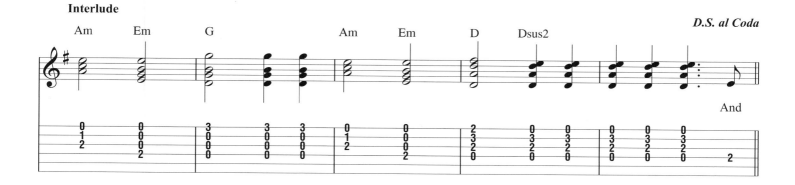

And

Coda

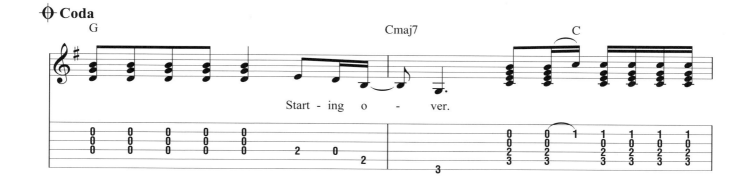

Start - ing o - ver.

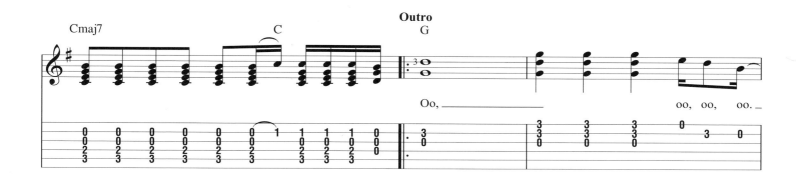

Outro

Oo, _____ oo, oo, oo. ___

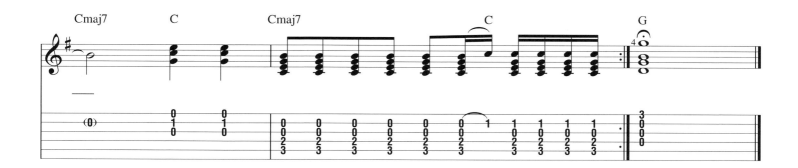

Additional Lyrics

2. This might not be an easy time.
   There's rivers to cross and hills to climb.
   Some days we might fall apart,
   And some nights might feel cold and dark.
   But nobody wins afraid of losin',
   And the hard roads are the ones worth choosin'.
   Someday we'll look back and smile,
   And know it was worth every mile.

Therefore I Am

Words and Music by Billie Eilish O'Connell and Finneas O'Connell

Strum Pattern: 2
Pick Pattern: 4

Chorus
Moderately slow

I'm not your friend, or an-y-thing. Damn, you think that you're the

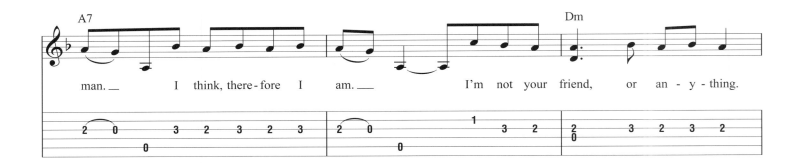

man. __ I think, there-fore I am. __ I'm not your friend, or an-y-thing.

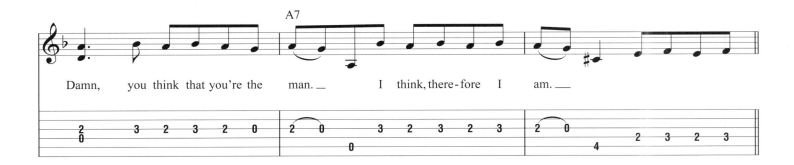

Damn, you think that you're the man. __ I think, there-fore I am. __

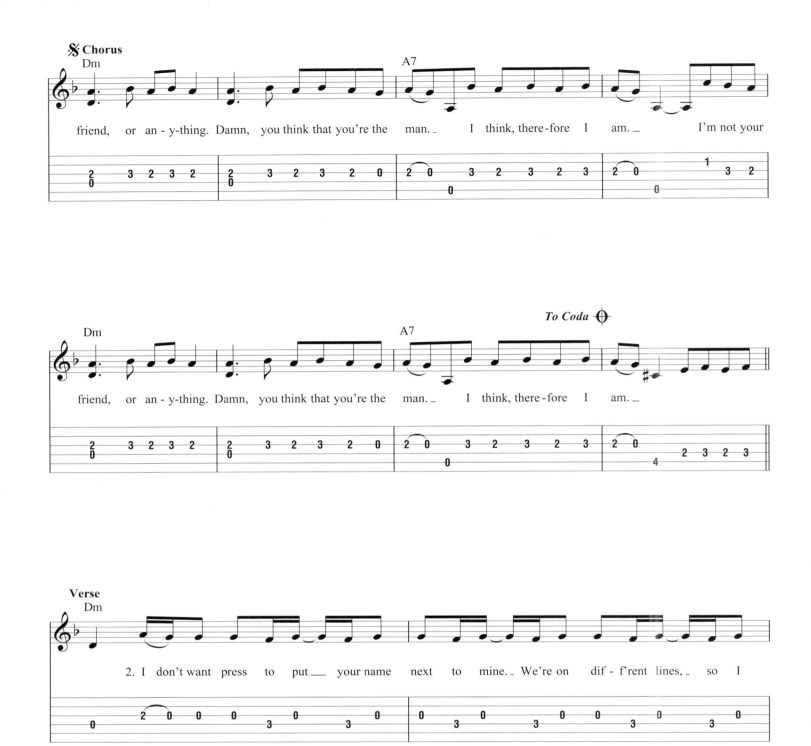

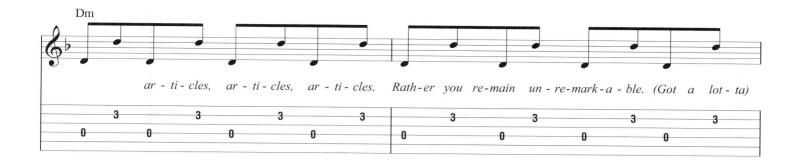

ar - ti - cles, ar - ti - cles, ar - ti - cles. Rath-er you re-main un - re-mark-a - ble. (Got a lot - ta)

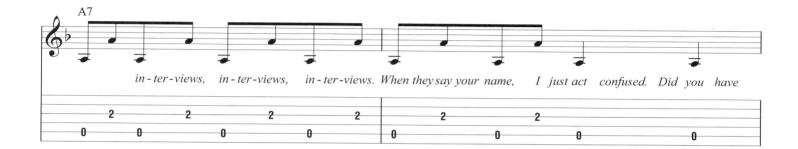

in - ter-views, in - ter-views, in - ter-views. When they say your name, I just act confused. Did you have

D.S. al Coda

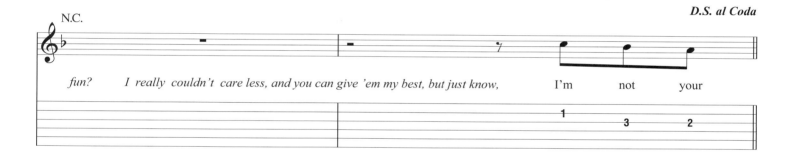

fun? I really couldn't care less, and you can give 'em my best, but just know, I'm not your

Coda

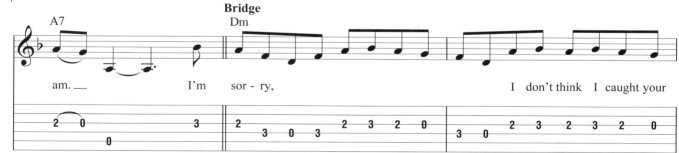

Bridge

am. __ I'm sor - ry, I don't think I caught your

name. I'm sor - ry,

I don't think I caught your name. _____

Interlude

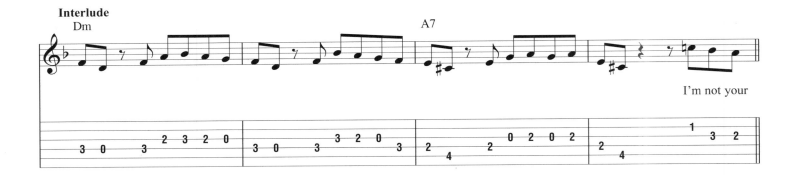

I'm not your

Outro-Chorus

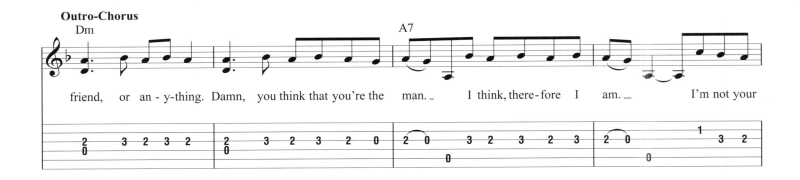

friend, or an-y-thing. Damn, you think that you're the man. __ I think, there-fore I am. __ I'm not your

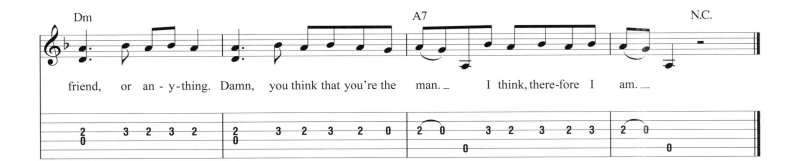

friend, or an-y-thing. Damn, you think that you're the man. __ I think, there-fore I am. __

Watermelon Sugar

Words and Music by Harry Styles, Thomas Hull, Mitchell Rowland and Tyler Johnson

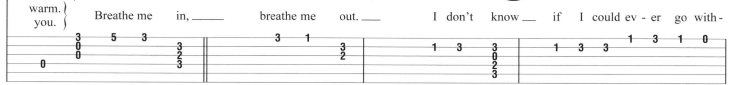

Strum Pattern: 3, 4
Pick Pattern: 3, 4

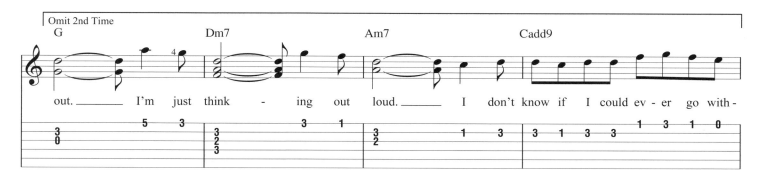

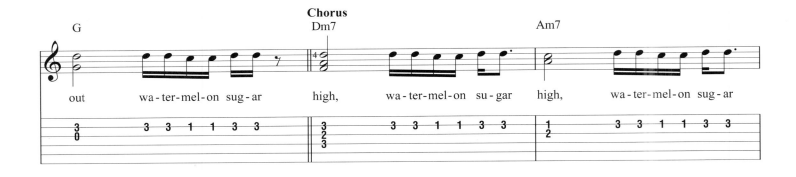

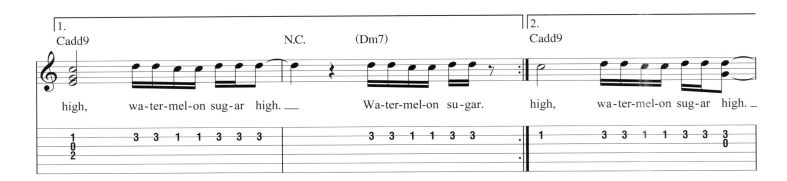

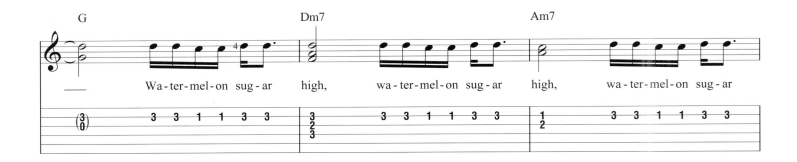

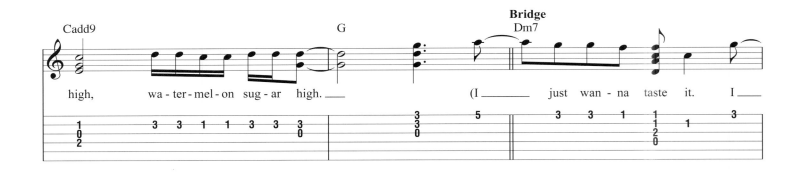

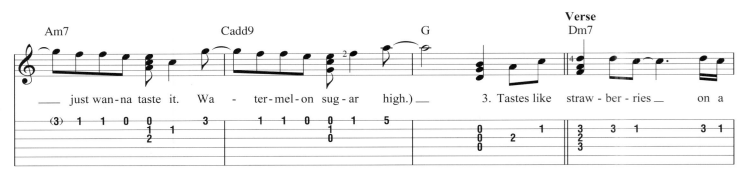

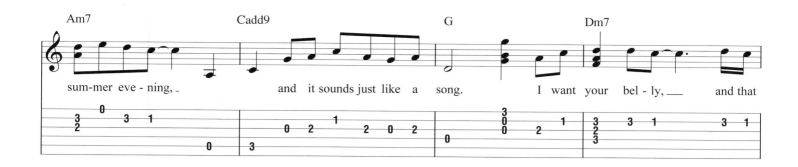

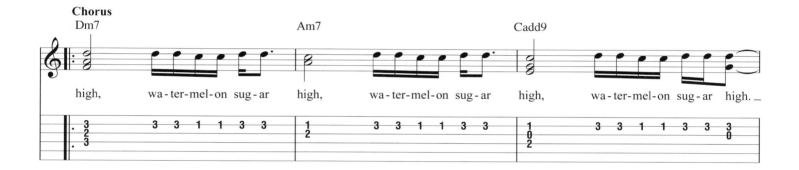

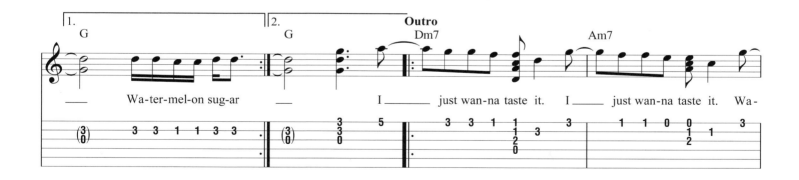

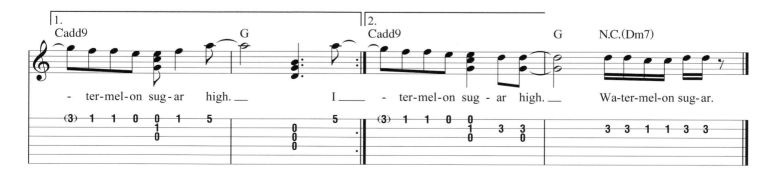

Willow

Words and Music by Taylor Swift and Aaron Dessner

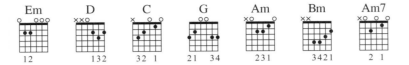

Strum Pattern: 3, 4
Pick Pattern: 3, 4

Intro
Moderately slow, in 2

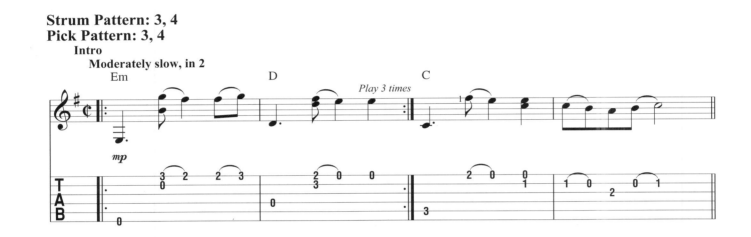

Play 3 times

§ Verse

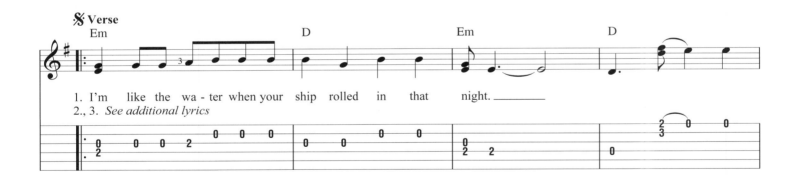

1. I'm like the wa-ter when your ship rolled in that night. _____
2., 3. *See additional lyrics*

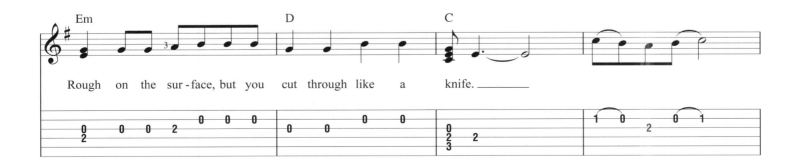

Rough on the sur-face, but you cut through like a knife. _____

*Chorus sung one octave higher.

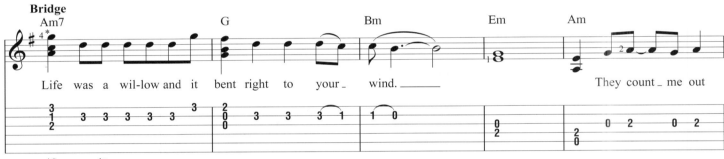

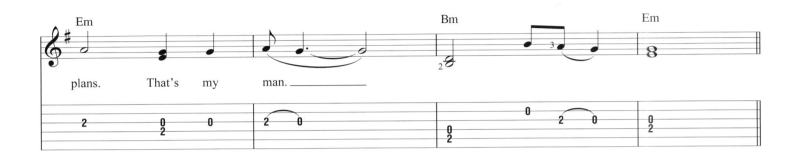

*Sung as written.

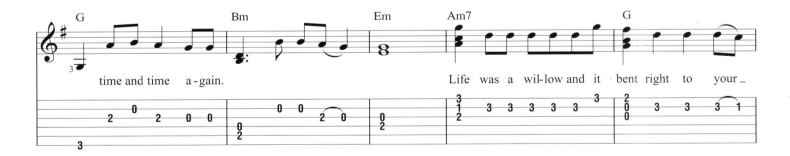

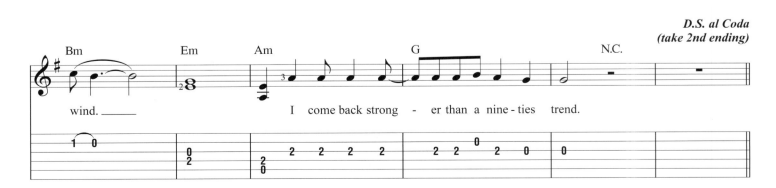

*Sung as written.

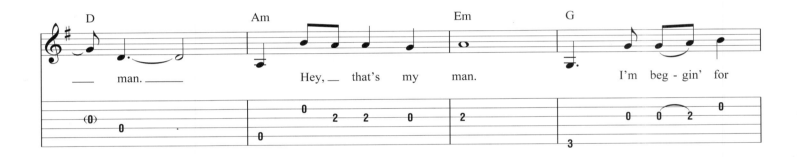

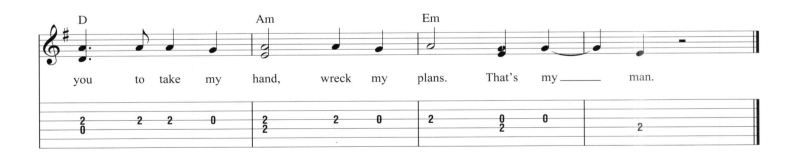

Additional Lyrics

2. Life was a willow and it bent right to your wind.
   Head on the pillow, I could feel you sneakin' in.
   As if you are a mythical thing,
   Like you were a trophy or a champion ring.
   And there was one prize I'd cheat to win.

3. Wait for the signal and I'll meet you after dark.
   Show me the places where the others gave you scars.
   Now this is an open-shut case;
   I guess I should-a known from the look on your face.
   Ev'ry bait and switch was a work of art.

You Broke Me First

Words and Music by Tate McRae, Blake Harnage and Victoria Zaro

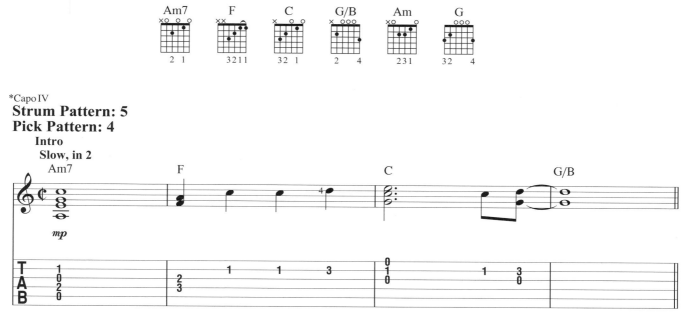

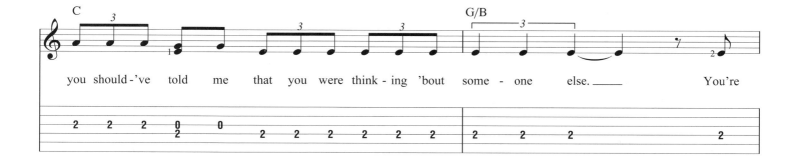

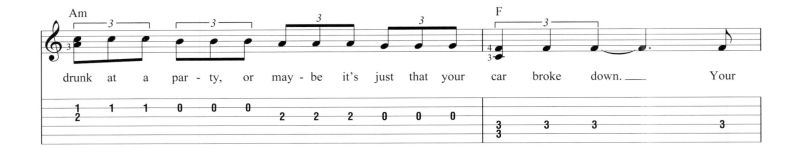

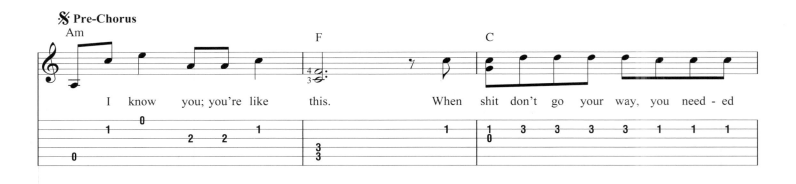

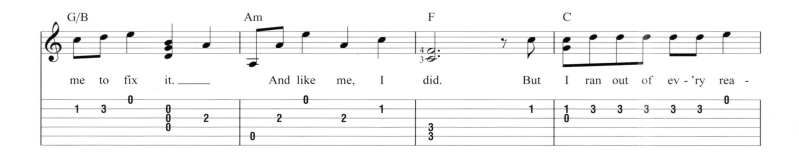

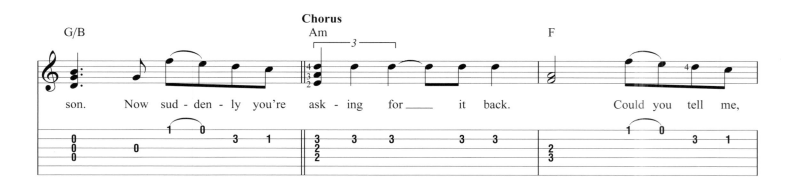

where'd you get ___ the nerve? Yeah, you could say you miss all that ___ we had,

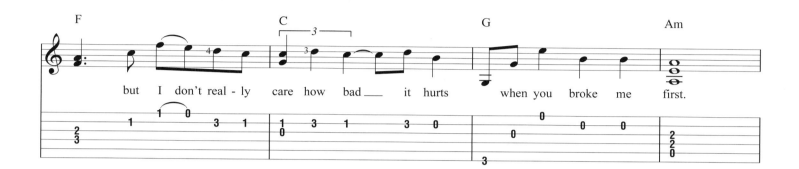

but I don't real - ly care how bad ___ it hurts when you broke me first.

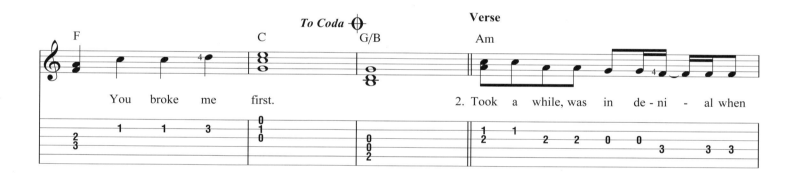

To Coda ⊕   **Verse**

You broke me first. 2. Took a while, was in de - ni - al when

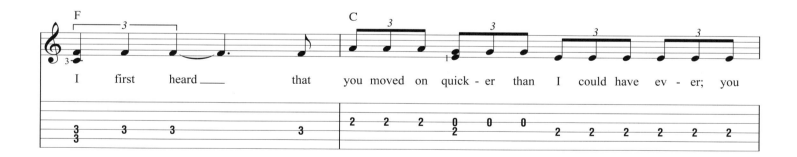

I first heard ___ that you moved on quick - er than I could have ev - er; you

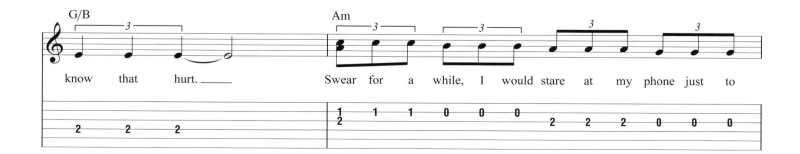

know that hurt. ___ Swear for a while, I would stare at my phone just to

see your name. ___ But now that it's there, I don't real-ly know what to say.

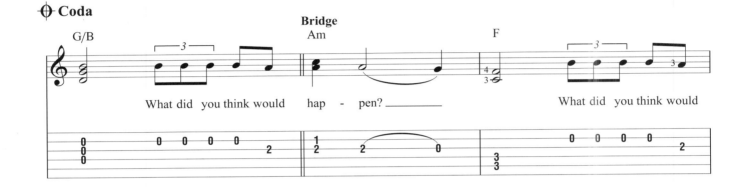

Coda

What did you think would hap - pen? ___ What did you think would

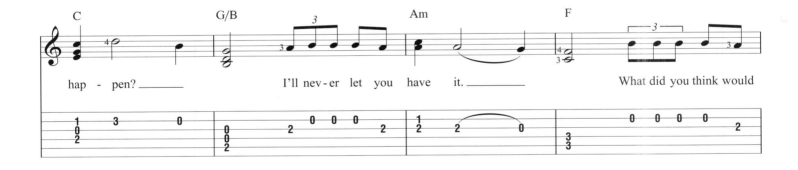

hap - pen? ___ I'll nev-er let you have it. ___ What did you think would

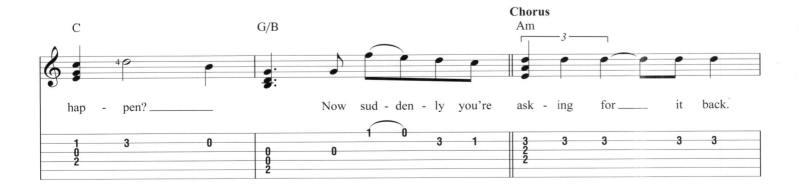

hap - pen? ___ Now sud-den-ly you're ask-ing for ___ it back.

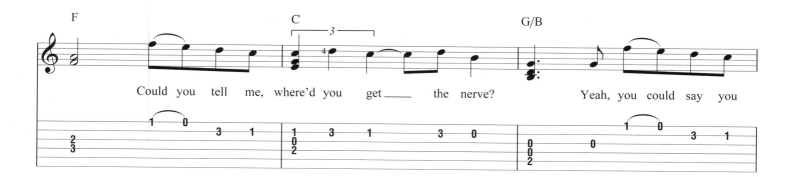

Could you tell me, where'd you get ____ the nerve? Yeah, you could say you

miss all that ____ we had, but I don't real - ly care how bad ____ it hurts

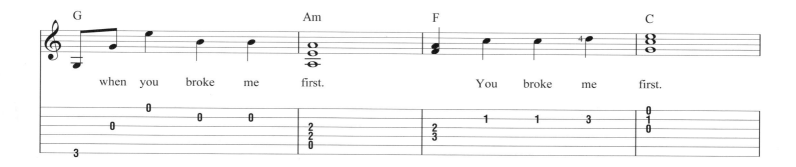

when you broke me first. You broke me first.

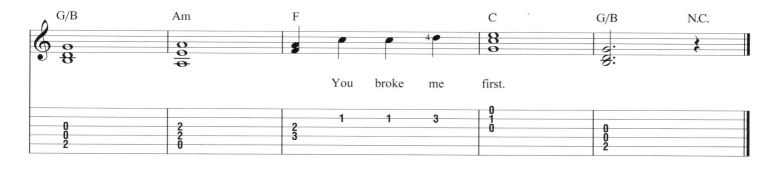

You broke me first.

EASY GUITAR WITH NOTES & TAB

This series features simplified arrangements with notes, tab, chord charts, and strum and pick patterns.

MIXED FOLIOS

00702287	Acoustic	$16.99
00702002	Acoustic Rock Hits for Easy Guitar	$15.99
00702166	All-Time Best Guitar Collection	$19.99
00702232	Best Acoustic Songs for Easy Guitar	$14.99
00119835	Best Children's Songs	$16.99
00702233	Best Hard Rock Songs	$15.99
00703055	The Big Book of Nursery Rhymes & Children's Songs	$16.99
00698978	Big Christmas Collection	$17.99
00702394	Bluegrass Songs for Easy Guitar	$12.99
00289632	Bohemian Rhapsody	$17.99
00703387	Celtic Classics	$14.99
00224808	Chart Hits of 2016-2017	$14.99
00267383	Chart Hits of 2017-2018	$14.99
00334293	Chart Hits of 2019-2020	$16.99
00702149	Children's Christian Songbook	$9.99
00702028	Christmas Classics	$8.99
00101779	Christmas Guitar	$14.99
00702185	Christmas Hits	$10.99
00702141	Classic Rock	$8.95
00159642	Classical Melodies	$12.99
00253933	Disney/Pixar's Coco	$16.99
00702203	CMT's 100 Greatest Country Songs	$29.99
00702283	The Contemporary Christian Collection	$16.99
00196954	Contemporary Disney	$19.99

00702239	Country Classics for Easy Guitar	$22.99
00702257	Easy Acoustic Guitar Songs	$14.99
00702280	Easy Guitar Tab White Pages	$29.99
00702041	Favorite Hymns for Easy Guitar	$10.99
00222701	Folk Pop Songs	$14.99
00126894	Frozen	$14.99
00333922	Frozen 2	$14.99
00702286	Glee	$16.99
00702160	The Great American Country Songbook	$16.99
00267383	Great American Gospel for Guitar	$12.99
00702050	Great Classical Themes for Easy Guitar	$8.99
00702116	Greatest Hymns for Guitar	$10.99
00275088	The Greatest Showman	$17.99
00148030	Halloween Guitar Songs	$14.99
00702273	Irish Songs	$12.99
00192503	Jazz Classics for Easy Guitar	$14.99
00702275	Jazz Favorites for Easy Guitar	$15.99
00702274	Jazz Standards for Easy Guitar	$17.99
00702162	Jumbo Easy Guitar Songbook	$19.99
00232285	La La Land	$16.99
00702258	Legends of Rock	$14.99
00702189	MTV's 100 Greatest Pop Songs	$24.95
00702272	1950s Rock	$15.99
00702271	1960s Rock	$15.99
00702270	1970s Rock	$16.99
00702269	1980s Rock	$15.99

00702268	1990s Rock	$19.99
00109725	Once	$14.99
00702187	Selections from O Brother Where Art Thou?	$19.99
00702178	100 Songs for Kids	$14.99
00702515	Pirates of the Caribbean	$16.99
00702125	Praise and Worship for Guitar	$10.99
00287930	Songs from *A Star Is Born, The Greatest Showman, La La Land,* and More Movie Musicals	$16.99
00702285	Southern Rock Hits	$12.99
00156420	Star Wars Music	$14.99
00121535	30 Easy Celtic Guitar Solos	$15.99
00702156	3-Chord Rock	$12.99
00702220	Today's Country Hits	$12.99
00244654	Top Hits of 2017	$14.99
00283786	Top Hits of 2018	$14.99
00702294	Top Worship Hits	$15.99
00702255	VH1's 100 Greatest Hard Rock Songs	$29.99
00702175	VH1's 100 Greatest Songs of Rock and Roll	$27.99
00702253	Wicked	$12.99

ARTIST COLLECTIONS

00702267	AC/DC for Easy Guitar	$15.99
00702598	Adele for Easy Guitar	$15.99
00156221	Adele – 25	$16.99
00702040	Best of the Allman Brothers	$16.99
00702865	J.S. Bach for Easy Guitar	$14.99
00702169	Best of The Beach Boys	$12.99
00702292	The Beatles — 1	$19.99
00125796	Best of Chuck Berry	$15.99
00702201	The Essential Black Sabbath	$12.95
00702250	blink-182 — Greatest Hits	$16.99
02501615	Zac Brown Band — The Foundation	$19.99
02501621	Zac Brown Band — You Get What You Give	$16.99
00702043	Best of Johnny Cash	$16.99
00702090	Eric Clapton's Best	$12.99
00702086	Eric Clapton — from the Album Unplugged	$15.99
00702202	The Essential Eric Clapton	$15.99
00702053	Best of Patsy Cline	$15.99
00222697	Very Best of Coldplay – 2nd Edition	$14.99
00702229	The Very Best of Creedence Clearwater Revival	$15.99
00702145	Best of Jim Croce	$15.99
00702219	David Crowder*Band Collection	$12.95
00702278	Crosby, Stills & Nash	$12.99
14042809	Bob Dylan	$14.99
00702276	Fleetwood Mac — Easy Guitar Collection	$16.99
00139462	The Very Best of Grateful Dead	$15.99
00702136	Best of Merle Haggard	$14.99
00702227	Jimi Hendrix — Smash Hits	$19.99
00702288	Best of Hillsong United	$12.99
00702236	Best of Antonio Carlos Jobim	$15.99

00702245	Elton John — Greatest Hits 1970–2002	$17.99
00129855	Jack Johnson	$16.99
00702204	Robert Johnson	$12.99
00702234	Selections from Toby Keith — 35 Biggest Hits	$12.95
00702003	Kiss	$16.99
00110578	Best of Kutless	$12.99
00702216	Lynyrd Skynyrd	$16.99
00702182	The Essential Bob Marley	$14.99
00146081	Maroon 5	$14.99
00121925	Bruno Mars – Unorthodox Jukebox	$12.99
00702248	Paul McCartney — All the Best	$14.99
00702129	Songs of Sarah McLachlan	$12.95
00125484	The Best of MercyMe	$12.99
02501316	Metallica — Death Magnetic	$19.99
00702209	Steve Miller Band — Young Hearts (Greatest Hits)	$12.95
00124167	Jason Mraz	$15.99
00702096	Best of Nirvana	$15.99
00702211	The Offspring — Greatest Hits	$12.95
00138026	One Direction	$14.99
00702030	Best of Roy Orbison	$16.99
00702144	Best of Ozzy Osbourne	$14.99
00702279	Tom Petty	$12.99
00102911	Pink Floyd	$16.99
00702139	Elvis Country Favorites	$17.99
00702293	The Very Best of Prince	$16.99
00699415	Best of Queen for Guitar	$15.99
00109279	Best of R.E.M.	$14.99
00702208	Red Hot Chili Peppers — Greatest Hits	$16.99
00198960	The Rolling Stones	$16.99
00174793	The Very Best of Santana	$14.99
00702196	Best of Bob Seger	$15.99

00146046	Ed Sheeran	$17.99
00702252	Frank Sinatra — Nothing But the Best	$17.99
00702010	Best of Rod Stewart	$16.99
00702049	Best of George Strait	$14.99
00702259	Taylor Swift for Easy Guitar	$15.99
00254499	Taylor Swift – Easy Guitar Anthology	$19.99
00702260	Taylor Swift — Fearless	$14.99
00139727	Taylor Swift — 1989	$17.99
00115960	Taylor Swift — Red	$16.99
00253667	Taylor Swift — Reputation	$17.99
00702290	Taylor Swift — Speak Now	$16.99
00702223	Chris Tomlin—Arriving	$16.99
00232849	Chris Tomlin Collection – 2nd Edition	$12.95
00702226	Chris Tomlin — See the Morning	$12.95
00148643	Train	$14.99
00702427	U2 — 18 Singles	$16.99
00702108	Best of Stevie Ray Vaughan	$16.99
00279005	The Who	$14.99
00702123	Best of Hank Williams	$15.99
00194548	Best of John Williams	$14.99
00702111	Stevie Wonder — Guitar Collection	$9.95
00702228	Neil Young — Greatest Hits	$15.99
00119133	Neil Young — Harvest	$14.99

Prices, contents and availability subject to change without notice.